Irish for Parents

Starter Book

www.askateacher.ie

Contents

Everyday Phrases

Conas atá tú?
Kun-ass ah taw too?
How are you?

Tá mé go maith.
Taw may guh mawh
I am good

Maidin maith
Maw-jin mawh
Good morning

Oíche mhaith
Ee-ha wah
Good night

An bhfuil tú ceart go leor?
Awn will too kyart guh lur?
Are you ok?

Slán
slawn
Goodbye

Dia duit
Dee-ah ditch
Hello to you

Dia is Muire duit
Dee-ah iss mwur-ah ditch
Hello back to you

Go raibh maith agat
Guh rev mawh ah-gut
Thank you

Tá failte romhat
Tae fall-cha roe-at
You're welcome

3

Laethanta na Seachtaine

Lay-han-ta nah shock-tan-ah

Days of the Week

An Luan
On Loo-in
Monday

An Mháirt
On Vart
Tuesday

An Chéadaoin
On Kay-deen
Wednesday

An Déardaoin
On Dare-deen
Thursday

An Aoine
On Een-na
Friday

An Satharn
On Sah-hern
Saturday

An Domhnach
On Dow-nok
Sunday

TODAY

Inniu An Luan
In-new on Loo-in
Today is Monday

Inniu _____
In-new_____
Today is _____

4

Doing words

Tá mé ____
Taw may ___
I am ____

ag gáire
egg goy-ra
laughing

ag rith
egg rih
running

ag ól
egg ole
drinking

ag damhsa
egg dow-sa
dancing

ag tafann
egg taw-fan
barking

Níl mé ____
Neel may ___
I am not ____

ag caoineadh
egg kwee-noo
crying

ag léamh
egg lay-ev
reading

ag ithe
egg ih-he
eating

ag scríobh
egg scree-uv
writing

ag caint
egg kine-t
talking

Bia

Bee-ah

Food

Is maith liom...

Iss mah lum

I like

Ní maith liom...

Nee mah lum

I don't like

Ba mhaith liom...

Buh wah lum

I would like

Im

im

Butter

Arán

Ah-rawn

Bread

Cáis

Kaw-sh

Cheese

Subh

S-uv

Jam

Bainne

Bawn-nya

Milk

Tósta

Toe-sta

Toast

Sú oráiste

Soo or-awsh-ta

Orange juice

Ispíní

Ish-peen-nee

Sausages

6

Cairéad
ka-rayd
Carrot

 **Tráta**
traw-ta
Tomato

 **Píotsa**
peet-sa
Pizza

 **Uisce**
ish-ka
Water

 **Cáca**
kaw-ka
Cake

 **ÚII**
ool
Apple

 **Sicín**
shik-een
Chicken

 Prátaí
praw-tee
Potatoes

 Pasta
Pasta

 Brioscaí
briss-kee
Biscuits

 Sceallóga
ska-low-ga
Fries/chips

 Anraith
an-rah
Soup

 Ceapaire
kyap-er-ah
Sandwich

 Piorra
peer-ah
Pear

 Iasc
ee-ask
Fish

 Ubh
uv
Egg

 Iógart
yo-gart
Yoghurt

 Criospaí
kris-pee
Crisps

Cé?
kay
Who?

Cá?
kaw
Where?

Cén fáth?
kayn faw
Why?

Ceisteanna
Kesh-ten-nah
Questions

Conas?
kun-nass
How?

Cathain?
kaw-hen
When?

Cad?
 kawd
What?

@askateacher.ie

Cén t-ám?
kayn tawm
What time?

Cé mhéad?
kay vayd
How many?

An bhfuil tú...?
on will too?
Are you...?

Cén?
kayn
Which?

Ag - To Have

Tá cóta agam
taw coe-ta ah-gum
I have a coat

Tá hata agat
taw hat-ah ah-gut
You have a hat

Tá bróga ag Lucy
taw broe-gah egg Lucy
Lucy has shoes

Tá carr aige
taw car egg-geh
He has a car

Tá rothar aici
taw ruh-hor ah-kee
She has a bike

Tá madra againn
taw mawd-rah ah-gwin
We have a dog

Tá criospaí agaibh
taw kris-pee ah-gwiv
You all have crisps

Tá cais acu
taw kawsh ah-koo
They have cheese

9

Tá sé fuar
Taw shay fur
It is cold

Tá sé grianmhar
Taw shay green-warr
It is sunny

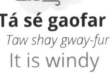

Tá sé gaofar
Taw shay gway-fur
It is windy

Aimsir
Am-sher
Weather

Tá sé scamallach
Taw shay skaw-meh-lock
It is cloudy

Tá sé ag cur báistí
Taw shay egg cur bawsh-tee
It is raining

Tá sé ag cur sneachta
Taw shay egg kur shnock-tah
It is snowing

Tá sé te
Taw shay teh
It is hot

Tá sé dorcha
Taw shay dur-ah-kah
It is dark

Tá sé stoirmiúil
Taw shay storm-ool
It is stormy

Tá an lá go breá
Taw on law guh brah
It is a fine day

Mé féin

May fayn
Myself

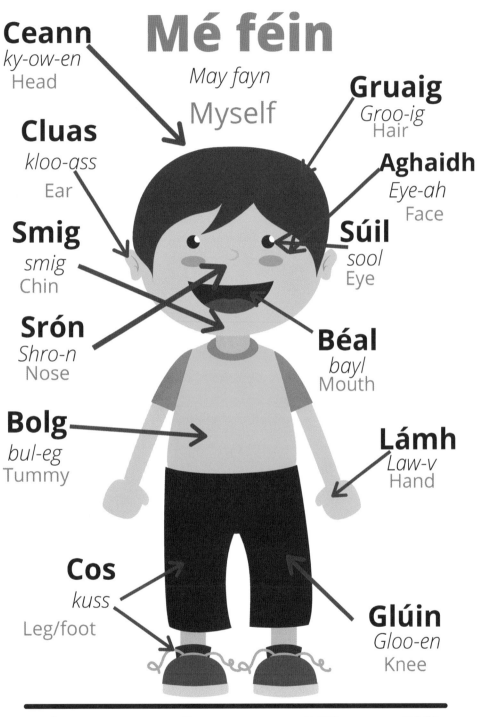

Ceann
ky-ow-en
Head

Cluas
kloo-ass
Ear

Smig
smig
Chin

Srón
Shro-n
Nose

Bolg
bul-eg
Tummy

Cos
kuss
Leg/foot

Gruaig
Groo-ig
Hair

Aghaidh
Eye-ah
Face

Súil
sool
Eye

Béal
bayl
Mouth

Lámh
Law-v
Hand

Glúin
Gloo-en
Knee

Cluasa	**Cosa**	**Súile**	**Glúine**
kloo-ass-ah	*kussa*	*soola*	*Gloo-en-ah*
Ears	Legs/feet	Eyes	Knees

Ar Scoil

Air skull

At School

Mála scoile
maw-la skull-ye
Schoolbag

Leabhar
l-ow-er
Book

Peann Luaidhe
p-yown loo-ee
Pencil

Cóipleabhar
cope-l-ow-er
copybook

Cathaoir
Caw-here
Chair

Scriosán
skriss-awn
eraser/rubber

Scuab
Skoo-ab
Brush

Páipéar
paw-pair
paper

Bord
Bord
Table

Bosca Lóin
Bus-ka Loe-n
Lunchbox

Múinteoir
Moon-chur
Teacher

Na hábhair

Nah haw-ver
The subjects

 **Gaeilge**
Gayl-gyah
Irish

 Ceol
Kyole
Music

 **Béarla**
Ber-lah
English

Eolaíocht
Ole-ee-ockt
Science

 **Stair**
Star
History

Ealaín
Al-een
Art

 **Mata**
Mata
Maths

Tíreolaíocht
Teer-ole-ee-ockt
Geography

 **Corpoideachas**
Korp-ij-a-kass
Physical Education

Creideamh
Kred-iv
Religion

Éadaí

Ay-dee

Clothes

Tá mé ag caitheamh...
Taw may egg kaw-hev

I am wearing...

T-léine
Tee lay-na
T-shirt

Geansaí
Gyan-zee
Jumper

Gúna
Goo-na
Dress

Bróga
Broe-gah
Shoes

Hata
Hat-ah
Hat

Stocaí
Stock-ee
Socks

Bríste
Breesh-te
Trousers

Seaicéad
Shack-aid
Jacket

Sciorta
Skur-ta
Skirt

Bróga reatha
Broe-gah rah-ha
Runners

Bríste gairid
Breesh-te gyar-ed
Shorts

Riteóga
Rih-toe-gah
Tights

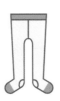

Culaith reatha
Kool-ah Rah-ha
Tracksuit

Sa Bhaile

Sah wall-ya

At home

Cistin

Kish-ten

Kitchen

Seomra suite

Show-mrah sitch-ah

Sitting room

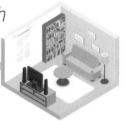

Seomra Folctha

Show-mrah full-ka

Bathroom

Garáiste

Gar-awsh-tah

Garage

Seomra bia

Show-mrah bee-ah

Dining room

Seomra codlata

Show-mrah kud-al-tah

Bedroom

Gairdín

Gar-jeen

Garden

Staighre

Sty-rah

Stairs

Caitheamh Aimsire

Kaw-hev am-sher

Hobbies/pastimes

Is breá liom...

Iss braw lum...

I love...

ag imirt leadóige

egg im-ert lad-oe-ge

playing tennis

ag snámh

egg snawv

swimming

ag imirt cispheile

egg im-ert kish-fell

playing basketball

ag imirt peile

egg im-ert pell-eh

playing football

ag damhsa

egg dow-sa

dancing

ag imirt rugbaí

egg im-ert rug-bee

playing rugby

ag péinteáil

egg paint-oil

painting

ag canadh

egg kawn-oo

singing

Teilifís
Tell-ah-feesh
Television

Tá _____ ar siúl ar an teilifís.
Taw _____ air shool air on tell-ah-feesh
_____ is on the television.

Nuacht
Noo-awkt
News

Clár grinn
Klawr grin
Comedy

Tráth na gceist
Traw nah gesht
Quiz show

Clár dúlra
Klawr dool-ra
Nature programme

Sobaldhráma
Sub-all draw-ma
Drama/soap

Clár spóirt
Klawr sport
Sports programme

Scannán
Skan-awn
Film

Clár cainte
Klawr kawn-cha
Talk show

17

Siopadóireácht

Shup-ah-door-awkt

Shopping

Cheannaigh mé...
Kyan-ig may...
I bought...

Consól cluichí
kon-sole klih-hee
Games console

Míreanna mearaí
Meer-ena mar-ee
Jigsaw

Leabhar
L-ow-er
Book

Liathróid
Leer-road
Ball

Téad scipeála
Tayd skip-awl-ah
Skipping rope

Cluiche cláir
klih-heh klawr
Board Game

Eitleog
Ech-lowg
Kite

Scútar
Skoo-tar
Scooter

18

Céard a fheiceann tú?

Kerd ah eck-en too?

What do you see?

Feicim....
Fek-im...
I see...

Carr
kar
car

Rothar
ruh-her
bike

Teach
t-yock
house

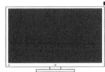 **Teilifís**
tell-ah-feesh
Television

 **Leaba**
lab-ah
Bed

 **Teidí**
ted-ee
Teddy

 **Babóg**
bah-boe-g
Doll

 **Doras**
dur-ass
Door

19

Ócáidí Speisialta

Oh-kawd-ee spesh-eel-ta

Special occasions

Oíche Shamhna
Ee-ha how-nah
Halloween

Nollag
Null-ig
Chistmas

Cásca

Kaw-ska
Easter

Lá Fhéile Pádraig
Law ay-la pawd-rig
St. Patrick's Day

Nollaig Shona Duit
Null-ig hunna ditch
Happy Christmas to you

Lá Breithe Shona Duit
Law breh-ha hunna ditch
Happy Birthday to you

Daidí na Nollaig
Dad-ee na null-ig
Santa

Na Míonna

Nah Mee-nah   The Months

Eanáir *Ann-er*   January

Feabhra *Fee-ow-rah*   February

Márta *Mar-ta*   March

Aibreán *Ab-rawn*   April

Bealtaine *Bee-yowl-ten-ah*   May

Meitheamh *Meh-hiv*   June

Iúil *Ool*   July

Lúnasa *Loon-ah-sa*   August

Meán Fómhair *Man fur*   September

Deireadh Fómhair *Jer-ah fur* October

Samhain *Sow-an*   November

Nollaig *Null-ig*   December

Uimhreacha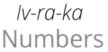

Iv-ra-ka

Numbers

When counting up numbers:

1	**A haon**	Ah hayn
2	**A dó**	Ah doe
3	**A trí**	Ah tree
4	**A ceathair**	Ah kah-hear
5	**A cúig**	Ah koo-ig
6	**A sé**	Ah shay
7	**A seacht**	Ah shawkt
8	**A hocht**	Ah hukt
9	**A naoi**	Ah nee
10	**A deich**	Ah jeh

Dearg
Jar-ag
Red

Buí
Bwee
Yellow

Gorm
Gor-um
Blue

Oráiste
Or-awsh-tah
Orange

Na Dathanna
Nah daw-han-ah
The Colours

Glas
Glawss
Green

Bándearg
Bawn-jar-ag
Pink

Dubh
Duv
Black

Donn
Dun
Brown

Corcra
Kor-kra
Purple

Ór
Ore
Gold

Liath
Lee
Grey

Bán
Bawn
White

23

Mé Féin agus Mo Rang

May fayn awg-us muh wrong
Myself and my class

Cad is ainm duit?
Kawd iss ann-im ditch?
What is your name?

Lucy is ainm dom
Lucy iss ann-im dum
My name is Lucy

Is mise Mark
Iss misha Mark
I am Mark

Cén rang in a bhfuil tú?
Kayn wrong in ah will too?
What class are you in?

Tá mé i naíonáin sóisearacha
Taw may ee nee-nawn so-ser-aka
I am in junior infants

Tá mé i naíonáin shinsearacha
Taw may ee nee-nawn shin-ser-aka
I am in senior infants

Tá mé i rang a haon/ dó/ trí/ ceathair/ cuig/ sé
Taw may ee wrong ah hayn/doe/ tree/ kah-her/ koo-ig/shay
I am in first/second/ third/ fourth/ fifth/ sixth class

Verbs - Past Tense

Chuaigh mé
Koo-ig may
I went

Chonaic mé
Kunick may
I saw

Rith mé
Rih may
I ran

Thosaigh mé
Huss-ig may
I started

Cheannaigh mé
Kyan-ig may
I bought

Léim mé
Laym may
I jumped

Scríobh mé
Shkree-uv may
I wrote

D'ith mé
Dih may
I ate

Chuir mé
Kur may
I put

Tháinig tú
Hawn-ig too
You came

Léigh tú
Lay too
You read (past)

Rinne tú
Rin-nah too
You made

D'ól sé
Dole shay
He drank

D'fhéach sé
Day-ock shay
He looked

Fuair sé
Fur shay
He got

D'óscail sí
Dusk-al shee
She opened

Bhí sí
Vee shee
She was

Chuala sí
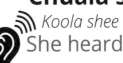 *Koola shee*
She heard

25

Mo Chlann
Muh klawn
My Family

Daideo
Dad-oh
Grandad

Mamó
Mam-oh
Granny

Aintín
Ant-cheen
Auntie

Uncail
Unk-al
Uncle

Mamaí
Mam-ee
Mammy

Daidí
Dad-ee
Daddy

Deartháir
Jer-hawr
Brother

Deirfiúr
Jer-fur
Sister

Col ceathrair

Kul Kah-rar
Cousin

Seanathair
Shan-ah-her
Grandfather

Seanmháthair
Shan-waw-her
Grandmother

Máthair
Maw-her
Mother

Athair
Ah-her
Father

Cá bhfuil teidí?

Caw will Teddy?

Where is teddy?

Tá teidí ar an gcathaoir.
Taw Teddy air on gaw-here.

Teddy is on the chair

Tá teidí sa chófra
Taw Teddy sah koe-fra.

Teddy is in the cupboard

Tá teidí faoin leaba
Taw Teddy fween lab-ah.

Teddy is under the bed

Tá teidí ag an doras
Taw Teddy egg on dur-ass

Teddy is at the door

Tá teidí in aice leis an mbosca
Taw Teddy in aka lesh on muska

Teddy is beside the box

Counting People

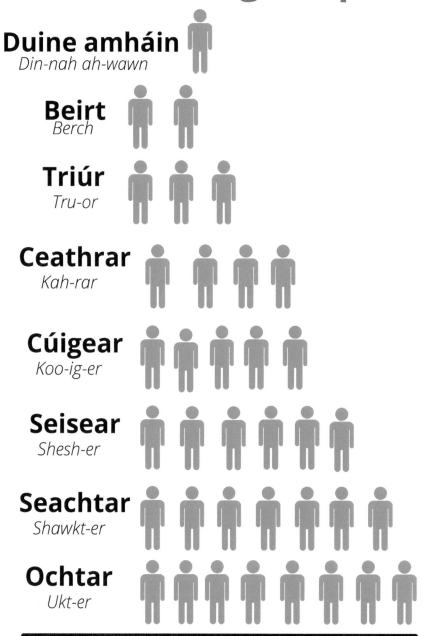

Duine amháin
Din-nah ah-wawn

Beirt
Berch

Triúr
Tru-or

Ceathrar
Kah-rar

Cúigear
Koo-ig-er

Seisear
Shesh-er

Seachtar
Shawkt-er

Ochtar
Ukt-er

<u>Cúigear</u> atá i mo theaghlach
Koo-ig-er ah taw i muh chiyg -lock
There are 5 people in my household

 **Tá**
Taw
Yes

Níl
Neel
No

An bhfuil tú?
On will too?
Are you?

Tá mé...
Taw may...
I am....

Níl mé...
Neel may...
I am not...

An raibh tú?
On rev too?
Were you?

Bhí mé...
Vee may...
I was....

Ní raibh mé...
Nee rev may...
I was not....

– –

An bhfuil tú fuar inniu?
On will too fur in-new?
Are you cold today?

Tá mé fuar inniu
Taw may fur in-new
I am cold today

An raibh tú te inné?
On rev too teh in-nyay?
Were you hot yesterday?

Ní raibh mé te inné
Nee rev may teh in-nyay
I was not hot yesterday

Tá ocras orm
Taw uck-rass ur-um
I am hungry

Tá tuirse orm
Taw tur-sha ur-um
I am tired

Tá tart orm
Taw tart ur-um
I am thirsty

Tá brón orm
Taw broe-n ur-um
I am sad

Tá áthas orm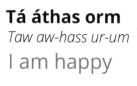
Taw aw-hass ur-um
I am happy

Tá eagla orm
Taw awg-la ur-um
I am scared

Tá fearg orm
Taw far-ug ur-um
I am angry

Tá tinneas orm
Taw tin-ass ur-um
I am sick

Tá fearg orm Me
Taw far-ug ur-um

Tá fearg uirthí She
Taw far-ug ur-hee

Tá fearg ort You
Taw far-ug urt

Tá fearg orainn We
Taw far-ug ur-in

Tá fearg air He
Taw far-ug air

Tá fearg oraibh You all
Taw far-ug ur-iv

Tá fearg orthu They
Taw far-ug ur-hoo

Try at Home

Cuir ort do chóta
Kur urt duh koe-tah
Put on your coat

Cuir ort do bhróga
Kur urt duh broe-gah
Put on your shoes

Scuab d'fhiacla
Skoob duh ee-ack-lah
Brush your teeth

Oscail an doras
Uss-kal on dur-ass
Open the door

Dún an fhuinneog
Doon on in-yoe-g
Close the window

Téigh a chodladh
Tay ah kull-ah
Go to sleep

Tá dinnéar réidh
Taw din-air ray
Dinner is ready

Cá bhfuil do mhála scoile?
Caw will duh wall-ah skull-ye?
Where is your school bag?

Main Sounds

Vowels

a = ah	e = eh	i = ih
á = aw	é = ay	í = ee
o = uh	u = uh	
ó = oh	ú = oo	

Two Consonants

ch = kah	bh = vah
fh = ih	dh = guh
mh = wuh	th = huh
sh = hew	

Silent letters

mb = b becomes silent

gc = c becomes silent

nd = d becomes silent

bp = p becomes silent

32

Go Raibh Maith Agat!

Guh rev mawh ah-gut!

Thank You!

I hope you have found this Irish Starter Book for parents useful.
I tried to make it user friendly, colourful and to cover the basics.

When teaching Irish, we cover 10 themes in school - Myself, School, Home, Hobbies/Pastimes, Television, Shopping, Clothes, Food, Weather and Special Occasions.

I have spelt each word out phonetically in order to pronounce the word correctly. With practice, you will pick up the proper sounds from the Irish words as you begin to notice patterns.

I really hope this helps you to build your confidence in Irish and maybe help with a little bit of homework!

Go n-éirí an t-ádh libh! (Guh nyigh-ree on taw liv)

Good luck to you all!
Sandra :)
www.askateacher.ie

Printed in Great Britain
by Amazon

42469630R00021